~Celebrity Influencers~

PHARRELL WILLIAMS

MARY HERTZ SCARBROUGH

Rourke Educational Media
A Division of Carson Dellosa Education
rourkeeducationalmedia.com

ROURKE'S **SCHOOL to HOME** CONNECTIONS

BEFORE AND DURING READING ACTIVITIES

Before Reading: *Building Background Knowledge and Vocabulary*

Building background knowledge can help children process new information and build upon what they already know. Before reading a book, it is important to tap into what children already know about the topic. This will help them develop their vocabulary and increase their reading comprehension.

Think about it...

1. Why do people enjoy paying attention to celebrities?
2. What is this celebrity famous for?
3. What are some of the qualities about celebrities that make them stand out?
4. What are the similarities and differences between a celebrity and a hero/heroine?
5. How does a person's professional career connect them to personal experiences?
6. How does what we know about the world shape the way we view ourselves?
7. How do our personal experiences shape our view of others?
8. How does the media shape our view of the world and ourselves?

Vocabulary: *Vocabulary Is Key to Reading Comprehension*

Use the following directions to prompt a conversation about each word.

- Read the vocabulary words.
- What comes to mind when you see each word?
- What do you think each word means?

Vocabulary Words:

- *anthem*
- *motivation*
- *obvious*
- *potential*
- *publicized*
- *upbeat*

During Reading: *Reading for Meaning and Understanding*

To achieve deep comprehension of a book, children are encouraged to use close reading strategies. During reading, it is important to have children stop and make connections. These connections result in deeper analysis and understanding of a book.

Close Reading a Text

During reading, have children stop and talk about the following:

- Any confusing parts
- Any unknown words
- Text to text, text to self, text to world connections
- The main idea in each chapter or heading

Encourage children to use context clues to determine the meaning of any unknown words. These strategies will help children learn to analyze the text more thoroughly as they read.

When you are finished reading this book, turn to the next-to-last page for **After Reading Questions** and an **Activity**.

Table of Contents

From One Hand to AnOTHER (FOHTA)

Pharrell Williams's goals extend far beyond his successes as a singer, songwriter, and producer. He wants "to change the world one kid at a time." His FOHTA foundation helps kids "meet their unique **potential**."

potential (puh-TEN-shuhl): what someone is capable of achieving in the future

333
Lewis Leathers
JAPAN
CDG

Pharrell started FOHTA in 2008. Success has a lot to do with opportunities, he realized. Young people who have the right tools are more likely to succeed. Technology, exposure to the arts, and having resources are all important.

The Importance of Resources
Pharrell's first program was a school supply giveaway. It was held in a park in his hometown in Virginia.

FOHTA focuses on science, technology, engineering, arts, mathematics, and **motivation** (STEAMM). It holds summer camps for elementary and middle schoolers. FOHTA started with one camp in Virginia. It now serves 1,700 kids and teens in six states.

motivation (MOH-tuh-vay-shuhn): the desire to accomplish something

A Helping Hand

The camps are free. Most kids come from low-income families or have other big challenges in their lives.

CUP1 W5

Campers often interact with scientists and other professionals. In 2018, campers in Virginia participated in a video chat with astronaut Alexander Gerst. He spoke from aboard the International Space Station.

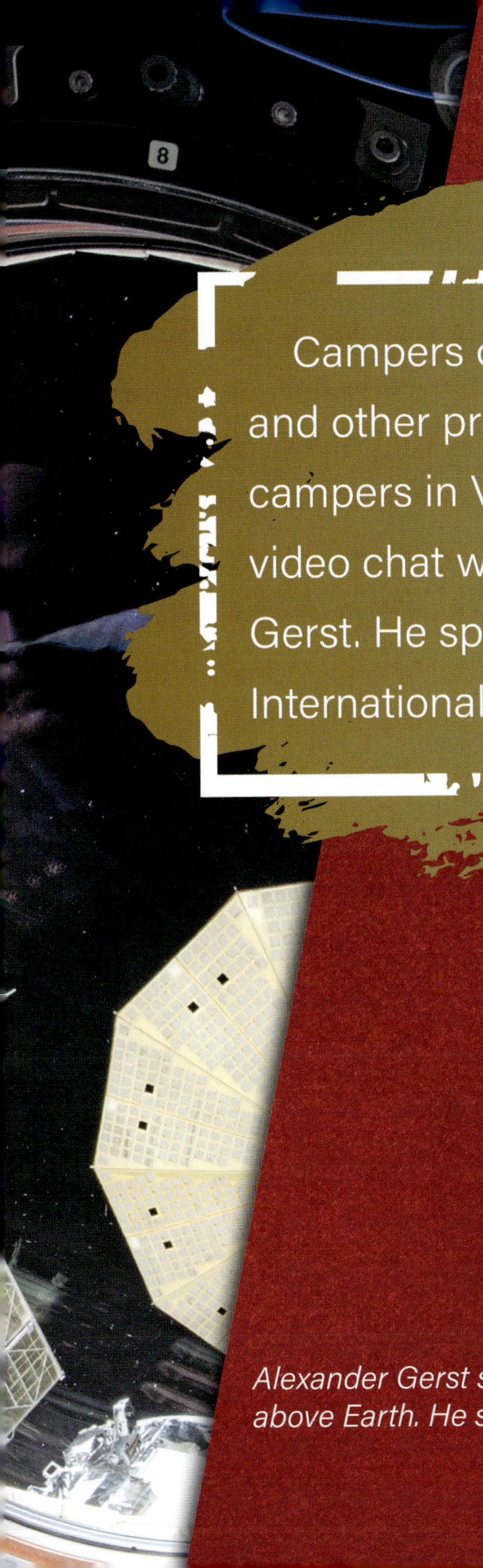

Tell Me More

Camps last for six weeks. Yoga, foreign languages, and potential careers are some of the things a camper might explore.

Alexander Gerst spoke to campers from 250 miles above Earth. He said we must take care of our home.

Pharrell opened his first camp in Virginia Beach, Virginia. He grew up there. He keeps giving back to his community. He also helped bring in a skate park and a learning center for technology and music.

Thanks, Mom!

Pharrell's desire to inspire others comes from his mom. She's a retired teacher and librarian. She helps run FOHTA.

More STEM, Please!

Pharrell helped produce the 2016 movie *Hidden Figures*. It is based on real African-American women who worked at NASA (the National Aeronautics and Space Administration). These mathematicians had critical roles in the United States space program in the 1960s. The movie **publicized** their little-known story.

More About *Hidden Figures*

- The women featured in the movie worked as "human computers."
- They battled discrimination and segregation.
- The movie was adapted from a nonfiction book.

publicized (PUHB-li-sizd): made known to as many people as possible

Pharrell released a STEM-inspired television series for teens and preteens. It came out in November 2018. The first 13 episodes of *Brainchild* examined topics such as space, memory, germs, creativity, and science in social media.

STEM stands for science, technology, engineering, and math.

Fascinated by Space

Pharrell appeared in an episode about space. He asked astronauts about the awe-inspiring things they've seen.

Pharrell's *Brainchild* show has plenty of funny parts. It also has a more serious, less **obvious** purpose. It is meant to encourage women and people of color to consider science careers.

obvious (AHB-vee-uhs): easy to see or understand

Happy Music

Pharrell's song "Happy" became an international hit in 2013 and 2014. Its **upbeat** tempo and catchy lyrics made people want to dance and sing along. It didn't have a deep message. "Happy" simply made people everywhere happy.

upbeat (UHP-beet): cheerful and optimistic

People around the world couldn't get enough of Pharrell's "Happy" song. They felt inspired to dance in the streets. They made their own versions of Pharrell's video. They posted them online. "Happy" kept spreading happiness.

#ReadHAPPY Book Giveaway

Pharrell published a kids' book. People posted about how reading makes them happy. Thousands of kids in need received free books.

Something unexpected happened after Pharrell's "Happy" song became popular. It became a protest **anthem**, or a call to action. The joyful music and dancing made a stark contrast with serious issues many faced. The song was a symbol for the human spirit.

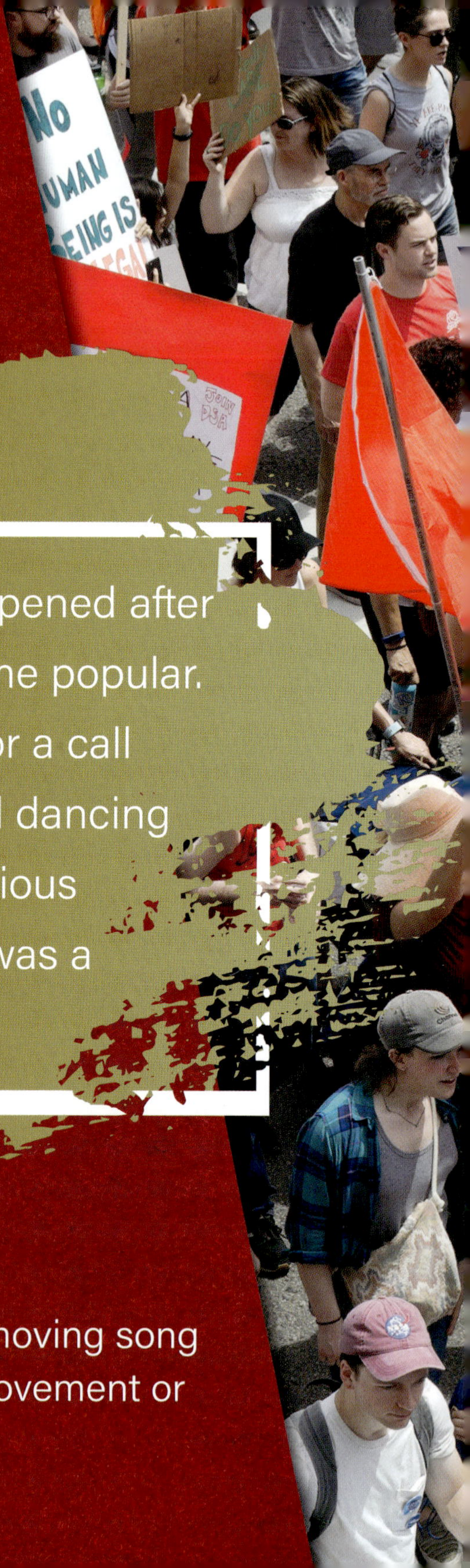

anthem (AN-thuhm): a spirited or moving song that is identified with a particular movement or point of view

Unhappy with the President

Pharrell sent U.S. President Donald Trump a letter. He said he did not support the president's controversial policies. Pharrell demanded that Trump stop playing "Happy" at his rallies.

Some "Happy" videos made by fans show protesters and police. People in the videos talk about wanting freedom.

Pharrell uses his platform to promote positivity. He helped spread happiness during the United Nations International Day of Happiness.

Pharrell urged people to celebrate the International Day of Happiness by taking action on climate change.

Pharrell uses his fame to lift others up. He has performed at the UNICEF Ball and at a show to benefit Children's Hospital Los Angeles. "How can we inspire," he asked, "if we are only behind the scenes?"

Memory Game

Look at the pictures. What do you remember reading on the pages where each image appeared?

Index

After Reading Questions

1. What are some topics a student could explore in one of Pharrell's summer camps?
2. How is Pharrell trying to change the world?
3. What are some things Pharrell thinks kids need to succeed?
4. What challenges did the women portrayed in *Hidden Figures* have to overcome?
5. What is a reason Pharrell created *Brainchild*?

Activity

Working with a partner or small group, watch some "Happy" videos made by people around the world to comment on political or cultural events. Pick one of the videos and do some further research. What is going on in that country or community that inspired people to make the video? What was the public reaction to the video? Use the internet to search for news articles. Then make a short presentation for others about the situation. Ask your audience for comments.

About the Author

Mary Hertz Scarbrough watched quite a few "Happy" videos while working on this book. She didn't get tired of the song or videos. She admires Pharrell's intellectual curiosity and would like to think she shares that trait with him. She loves researching and then writing about inspiring people.

www.rourkeeducationalmedia.com

PHOTO CREDITS - Cover: ©Twocoms/Shutterstock; p.5, 30: ©Anthony Mooney/Shutterstock; p.6-7, 28-29, 30: ©FatCamera; p.8-9: ©PeopleImages; p.8-9, 30: courtesy of European Space Agency; p.12-13: ©Merkuri2; p.14-15, 30: ©NASA/Kim Shiflett; p.16-17: ©Wavebreakmedia; p.18-19: ©Ranta Images; p.20-21, 30: ©ViewApart; p.22-23, 30: ©Paolo Pardiso; p.24-25: ©jferrer; p.26-27: ©W8 Photography/Shutterstock

Edited by: Kim Thompson
Cover and interior design by: Rhea Magaro-Wallace

Library of Congress PCN Data

Pharrell Williams / Mary Hertz Scarbrough
(Celebrity Influencers)
ISBN 978-1-73161-730-9 (hard cover)
ISBN 978-1-73161-266-3 (soft cover)
ISBN 978-1-73161-742-2 (e-Book)
ISBN 978-1-73161-754-5 (ePub)
Library of Congress Control Number: 2019932367

Rourke Educational Media
Printed in the United States of America,
North Mankato, Minnesota